The Society of
CLASSICAL POETS

Mount Hope, New York

Table of Contents

Introduction

Why You Should Be Reading Poetry

By Evan Mantyk

MEETING someone new and engaging him in friendly conversation, I explain, "I help run a poetry website." What follows is a general phenomenon I've observed in which the new acquaintance's eyes instantly lose their look of awareness and brilliance and adopt a glazed over impassivity that might be summarized as disinterest.

This phenomenon seems logical enough given the kaleidoscopic array of apparently better ways to communicate ideas with words or images, such as online videos, social media, movies, news and magazine articles and opinions, short stories, novels, and comic strips. With all of that, what does poetry have to offer and why should people today be reading it? Hasn't poetry been naturally rendered obsolete?

My answer: Not so! Simply put, poetry can make your life wonderful, beautiful, and awesome more fully and effectively than any of the above. "How can that be?" you may be asking, "Poetry is slower, engages fewer senses, often employs obscure knowledge and language, and provides a narrow view into only one person's feelings." I'll address the former two issues first.   The   aversion to poetry, and the feelings of slowness and sensory deprivation that it appears to induce, are exactly the symptoms of a sickness of our modern world, where attention spans and senses are constantly being diminished by artificial and commercial pressures to be more stimulating and exciting in our communication. Even old movies from a decade or two ago can seem unexciting and unfulfilling compared to the latest fast-paced blockbuster. However, if you can force yourself to slow down, quiet your mind, and really read a poem, then your consciousness is gaining what it unwillingly lost. The process is a subtle and subconscious transformation not easily quantified (although I would dare social scientists to try).

Just take a look at the enduring works of early 19th century English writer Jane Austen. What is so charming and delightful about her Romantic novels? In my view, there is a layer of civility and a sense of what is proper that coats everything in her works, so much so that—as in the case of *Pride and Prejudice*—a man may talk with a woman at length and on many occasions and still be unsure if she is fond of him since they are both acting out such elaborate rituals of kindness and humanity as expected of them by society. Should he propose? Should he spend his time elsewhere? Either way, it seems a splendid experience for all parties involved. All of the carefully rendered characters are acting in accord with society's assigned roles for them (with occasional deviation only creating a slight yet engrossing dissonance). It is a simple and appealing way of life. It is also attractive because it is so real. The world was undeniably simpler before industrialization set in, when there was more emphasis on nature, imagination, and intuition. Who wouldn't like the straightforward world of Jane Austen without leaving the comfort of their televisions or computers?

Thus, after 200 years, Austen continues to instill a sense of wonder and beauty that has led to an endless string of TV mini-series and movies—including, perhaps sadly, *"Pride and Prejudice and Zombies,"* due out this year. Her works are not poetry and neither is poetry prominently featured, although poetry is occasionally discussed. It is in the background in her novels and is taken for granted to be a pervasive part of the culture. Instead of movie and music stars, the entertainment superstars of the age were Romantic poets like Sir Walter Scott, William Wordsworth, Lord Byron, John Keats, and Percy Bysshe Shelley. Being able to slow your mind and senses down to enjoy true poetry is to enter into the charming and delightful mindset of Austen more fully than you can by actually reading her books or watching film adaptations. It is to enter into the grand and elaborate play that is humanity and society, to suddenly open your eyes and realize that you are on a vast stage and playing a role especially and benevolently written for you. How splendid!

I return now to the latter criticisms of poetry in general that I earlier listed: "often employs obscure knowledge and language, and provides a narrow view into only one person's feelings." These are very real and valid criticisms as far as poetry today is concerned. Most poetry today is written as if to be intentionally hard to understand and often employs no standard meter or rhyme. In fact, it is just creative prose being presented as poetry. Such abstruse and now hackneyed poetry essentially disregards the traditions of English poetry that have been laid for the last 1,400 years—traditions which themselves have built on Greek traditions, and more recently Chinese traditions, going back about 3,000 years. This is why the Society is collecting modern verse that looks and reads like poetry. It is reviving poetry that is clear and appealing to all of humanity, including people who may not have four years of college and those who do not "give a crap" about modern literary analysis.

This authenticity is the real challenge for poets today and the Society of Classical Poets accepts this confrontation with grace and gusto. In short, real poetry is a wonderful diversion worth tuning your mind to, and what is presented at the Society of Classical Poets is exactly the type of poetry I feel you will enjoy!

Section I

Beautiful & Sublime

"Niagara Falls, from the American Side," by Frederic Edwin Church, 1867.

Meryl Stratford

Helen Keller at Niagara Falls

SHE could not see the avalanche cascade
from foam-flecked marble rapids, being blind,
but torrents of egrets and apple blossoms played
whirlpools of nebulous beauty in her mind.
She could not hear, tumultuous mystery,
the thunderous plunge, a sea's storm-breaking crests,
crescendo of a choral symphony,
only the silence when the music rests.
But the earth beneath her trembled. She could feel
a power like perseverance, truth, or love,
the joyous lifting of a bridal veil,
a thirst fulfilled, the mist, the memory of
her teacher's cool, wet fingers like a brand,
burning that first word *water* in her hand.

Jane Blanchard

Bewintered

WHEN snow arrives
As long forecast,
It sets a scene
That does not last;

But for the while
Snow sits around,
All else remains
Transfixed, spellbound.

Fern G. Z. Carr

In the Shadow of a Mountain

IN the shadow of a mountain
lies a valley, lies my home

swaddled by the earth's embrace
in sweet repose – a state of grace

in the shadow of a mountain
in a valley, in my home

where I am blind to turquoise skies
blind to the clouds wafting by

in the shadow of a mountain
in the valley where I lie

my bones beneath the verdant sod
closer to the stars and God.

Abigail Zhong

The Shore

FOREVER lost in the ocean
the water seeps into my chest
I've lost myself in the motion
let the fish swim beneath my breast

And yet each time I'm pulled under
the sun too far to touch my face
never does my body sunder
and crumple in the sea's embrace

my lungs—they fight and swear and shout
until my mouth gasps in fresh air,
choking filthy salt water out
with the remnants of my despair

the ocean is all that I know
But I will make it to the shore
I'll swim until sand piles below
And tired feet touch solid floor

Mike Ruskovich

The River Wye

YOUR stroll beside the stream has stayed with me,
Has left me in my loneliness with strength
Enough to face the world, to somehow see
Within its depth and width and wandering length
The Truth that Keats and Coleridge saw with eyes
Romantic yet as real as river stones
That roll the water, washing clean the lies
That cling like greed to human flesh and bones.
Your words, worth all the days and nights I spend
In contemplation seeking my own worth,
Are currents catching me each time I bend
My back to labor, sifting through the Earth
You sorted for me walking by the Wye,
In lines admiring how instead of why.

Cathy Bryant

Fog in the Valley

THE fog flows down like a flock of pale gulls
and the valley of my home disappears.
In seconds, stuff engulfs us. Each sense dulls;
cold soggy cotton fills our eyes and ears.
And where now is Man's brilliance and pride?
Nature in a moment smothered it all.
Of all we have done, nothing now abides.
We stumble, helpless, through the silent pall.
But fog is much more merciful than Man.
It floats away, greeting the morning sun.
All we have is reborn, as if to plan.
We smile and get on; there's much to be done.
So Nature shows us her staggering power
but relents, as sweet as her smallest flower.

Shari Jo LeKane-Yentumi

Monarch

THEY gathered softly in a field for many miles around
to taste in haste the flowers before showers tumbled down
upon the clover blooms, the goldenrod, thistles and grasses;
never in one place too long as hungry blackbird passes.

An undulating wave of black and orange fills the skies.
Silent as a fairy, painted masterpiece that flies
on wings so paper thin, who could begin to realize
the journey and the magnitude for creatures of their size.

Locations to migrate are as innate as procreation.
From Canada to Mexico and through our very nation,
the Monarch is a royal, truly loyal to its subjects
in all of North America; to this, no one objects.

So, when I see the King float on his wings alone and stray,
just nosing in my garden on a lazy summer day,
I know he's on hiatus as a weary renegade,
for somewhere on their journey flies the whole Monarch
   Brigade.

Bruce Dale Wise

The Catskill Mountains
By Ubs Reece Idwal
From the pages of Washington Irving

WHOEVER's made a voyage up the Hudson must
remember Catskill Mountains, a dismembered branch
of the great Appalachian family, I trust.
West of the river, swelling to a noble chance,
their hues and shapes are magical barometers.
When weather's fair, they're clothed in blue and purple
  dance.
They print their outlines bold on Earth's thermometers,
against the clear and lovely, cloudless evening skies,
about to be explored by keen astronomers.
But sometimes they will gather vapors of great size,
in hoods of gray, about their summits, in the dusk;
and in the sunset's rays, their crowns of glory rise.

He Kept On
By Erisbawdle Cue

HE kept on striving to attain an ideality
connected to the good, but grounded in reality.
He kept on working to achieve perfection in the act,
pragmaticism on the run with satisfaction's fact.
He kept on pressing to combine both ecstasy and truth,
to do so now, as an adult, as he had done in youth.
He kept it up—this quest for love of knowledge and the true.
He longed to have it deep inside, so beautiful and new.
He kept on reaching to obtain more power all the time.
He longed to rise upon time's wings and felt it worth the
  climb.

Mandy Moe Pwint Tu

Morning Song

O SWEET be this soft morning's song
As golden mist on earth descends
And skylarks trill an hour long
While gently this wild river bends:

The daisies rise to kiss the sun
Fond lover of dear Mother Earth!
For now the war with night is won
What better cause for joy and mirth?

Courting the flowers, the butterflies
Drink deep of sweetest nectar-dew:
While pixies watch with peering eyes
A scene that never would be new:

The squirrels scurry up the trees
And chitter-chatter though the day:
And out upon the greenest lees
I might espy the deer at play!

Music of melodious note
Doth grace this breezy morning air –
Like madrigals that Pan devotes
To Mother Nature's glory fair!

O sweet is this soft morning's song
Which falls upon my eager ears:
As thrushes trill an hour long
I find dispelled my foolish fears!

Seasong

I HEARD the wreathéd coral horn
That Triton blew, and less forlorn
 Did suddenly I feel:
I heard the sirensong afar
I launched a ship and tracked a star
 How soon my heart did heal!

I saw the shade of Hy Brasil,
And what delight within me filled
 To find the Faery-land!
I would have halted, but the mists
Did swirl and whirl and coil and twist
 'Round the perilous strand.

On I sailed, under lonely skies
Under lonely stars that winked their eyes
 And watched me at the helm:
The sea, a lonely maiden, sighed
And whispered soft her empty lies
 That fooled this mortal realm.

The sea is a maiden, they say
Unpredictable, night or day
 Trust not her smiling face;
Loneliness is a mask she wears,
Mystery is the crown she bears
 But in her heart, there's rage.

I thought I drowned, and in a dream
I saw a great serpentine queen
 Who lived under the sea;
And then I heard the mermaid's song,
And listened to it an hour long
 For she did sing for me.

Her song was of pain and sorrow,
Of love that n'er saw the morrow,

And tears that long were wept;
And in a thousand stars she saw
Written an invisible door
    That I had never mapped.

Her love had wings, she sang, he flew
Into that starry door of blue
    And never did return:
Although she called his name that night
And waited 'till the dawn's first light
    Upon her pale face burned.

Then her tone did change to anger,
Then I heard the sound of thunder
    Clapping in the distance;
And maddened, she did shout and scream,
I was afeared, though 'twas a dream,
    Then she uttered silence.

Now I heard the sirens calling,
And I heard the sea-gods brawling
    Over some fickle thing;
Proteus, I saw him transform
From a seal into a man, adorned
    With shells and seaweed strings.

My eyes did open; I awoke
To the dawn that new had broke
    East of the wailing sea;
Upon the shore my head did rest
I rose and gazed into the west
    Where foam and spray danced free.

Triton's horn sounded, and the Star
Beckoned to me from leagues afar,
    The Sea herself did sing
The strain of some familiar tune
That once I heard beneath the moon
    Now in my heart did ring.

James Smith

A Spring Gathering

Haiku

EARLY spring beings,
A pulsing celebration,
In the night, they sing.

Evan Mantyk

Zhen-Shan-Ren
(Truth-Compassion-Forbearance)

ZHEN-Shan-Ren,* Zhen-Shan-Ren, Zhen-Shan-Ren!
The sound of the drums that beat in heaven,
Pounding out in a celestial rhythm,
Epic, elegant, enlightening hymn:
Zhen-Shan-Ren, Zhen-Shan-Ren, Zhen-Shan-Ren…

Even if heard by the lowest of men,
It can make their minds and their hearts ascend
With just one beat, one peek at this one trend:
Zhen-Shan-Ren, Zhen-Shan-Ren, Zhen-Shan-Ren…

What brilliance in the hearts of our children,
Who by nature are so simple and pure;
The thump of their quick little feet concur:
Zhen-Shan-Ren, Zhen-Shan-Ren, Zhen-Shan-Ren…

The sound resounds across a sea of sin;
Suddenly true thoughts, old dreams, awaken;
The way is clear to a home forgotten:
Zhen-Shan-Ren, Zhen-Shan-Ren, Zhen-Shan-Ren…

The blocked third eye may be pummeled open;
Sights so amazing, dazzling, and puzzling!
Even the rocks are alive and pulsing:
Zhen-Shan-Ren, Zhen-Shan-Ren, Zhen-Shan-Ren!

* *Pronounced "juhn-shahn-ren": the three main principles of the meditation practice Falun Dafa, also known as Falun Gong.*

New Tang Poets

Haiku

ANCIENT poets speak,
Fresh air gently wafts right in
From the mountain's peak.

Evening

Haiku

THE lake's voices chirp
Beneath a warm dark curtain,
Tea is softly slurped.

Untitled

AS the warm day winds on, I find myself
Studying the Buddha's Law a second time.
There is work piled upon my desk and shelf;
Problems solve themselves when in the sublime.

A Bud of Spring

I LOOK upon a bud of spring and dwell
"Is your journey through depths of suffering
Through the vicissitudes of wintry hell
Worth your tiny not quite green offering?
You are but a penitent, lone and meek
Confined for your short life you'll always be
To this rigid branch, not that high, quite weak,
To be alive but never to be free."

The tiny bud, more alive than I thought,
Shakes its bulbous head in the gentle breeze
And, in language that can't be figured out
But can be felt and clearly known with ease,
To me speaks: "How shallow is your vision;

I'm not a single bud, I am a tree,
But not the single tree you imagine,
All maple trees together that is me;
Yet, if they are all dead, I still exist,
I am the perfect tree, the King of Trees;
How does a small seed grow and not desist,
How does it grow with such form and ease?
Because in my Realm, it's already there,
A piece of my vast body eons old,
And yet my body is in fact right here,
If you can free your mind, you will behold."

On hearing this I feel myself expand,
My body, like a flesh and bone robe
Darkly wrinkled in a gripping hand,
Released, it spreads upon our tiny globe.

Spreads beyond stars that lord over the night,
And wavelengths my eyes are accustomed to,
Beyond emotions of fright and delight,
Beyond shallow concepts of what is true.

There, in a sea of endless life and light,
Floating, I meet the King of Trees once more,
I say, "Then it's all real and you are right,
Remind me next time I am such a boor!"

A Moon Poem

For the Mid-Autumn, or Moon, Festival

MY Ford Explorer ascends no higher
Only making it half up the first hill
On a December night cold and dire,
The truck, that old machine, loses its will.

Not I, I spring forth and rustle about,
Fitting spikes on my boots for the climb

Up the mountain where rain has frozen stout—
My spikes, a nice thought, break off in no time.

It's not all bad, the moon lights up my way;
It leaves just enough purple blue softness
So that I know that I won't ever stray,
Even if I can't see my feet in darkness.

Taking baby steps, my fate is unsure,
Yet, I smile at this moonlit adventure.

The Chain

Upon a Marriage

ONE hand reaches for another,
It grasps tight in the fast current,
Each one's arm is linked together,
Each finger locked and diligent.

The human chain swerves to and fro,
It reaches out to those swept away
In the stream's turgid manic flow
Distressed eyes are withered and gray.

The chain plucks out those who it can;
It takes them to safe and firm land,
On the moral fiber of man,
On solid character you can stand.

Oh no! One link has been broken!
A gap near the tip of the chain
Is now fatally sprung open;
It burst apart amidst the strain.

Behold! What's that? A golden light!
Someone new appears from upstream:
She grabs one hand fast with her right,
The left is too far so it seems.

Across from her, he stretches out
To reconnect the broken chain;
So piercing the pain, he wants to shout,
No time to think or to complain.

He only knows it can't be hewed,
The one long hope must not sever,
The link is made, the quest renewed!
The chain is longer than ever.

Reid McGrath

Tares in the Wheat

"The sun will burn; the heat will cause you sweat;
Dust will choke before the sun is set,"
—Michael Curtis, "Novice"

WHEN I recall various seeds I've sown
I'm prone to clench my teeth and tug my hair.
I look back on the lea and it looks bare.
My bag of seed was by the devil blown
chock-full of tares, not wheat, misleading plants:
Green at first but browning on the easel.
I'm upset; but relieved that it's legal
to change my name, or move, or to supplant,
to start afresh and bury the old crap,
is comforting. I keep my eyes ahead,
on the offing, tighten the safety strap,
and press on plowing till I'm spent and dead.
The juvenile weeds were a mishap.
From now on (try!) I'll make Prudence my friend.

A Recurring Dream, Vanquished

I HAD a nightmare when I was a boy
with animals at first docile and sweet,
with tie-dyed leaves which were like cruel decoys
distracting me from what I was to meet…
A bright, autumnal tunnel would transform
to craggy scene of blacks and shark-gray blues,
one blasted tree-trunk and a thunder storm,
a Sea of Death and all its darkening hues!

I amble down another sylvan path
and all about me the umbrageous trees

display colors that make me want to laugh;
or say a thankful prayer upon my knees.
For now, when I have reached this Cliff of mine,
the Terror's altered: I see the Sublime.

Retreating Snow

LIKE an old man dragging his long white hair
out of the lawn, back toward the forest's shade,
the snow retreats, cornered, and well-aware
of time that's up and warmth it can't evade…

Young blonde Apollo bays this crumbling foe
and inch by inch reclaims the tawny grass;
and while there is a time for fresh-white snow,
one does exclaim: "At last! At last! At last!"

His Palomino team touch on the ground
and pull their pony-cart over the fields
spreading their burlap-color all around;
tan Phoebus*, with his long-bow that he wields,
steals back the landscape, conquers the old snow,
which soon enough will have nowhere to go.

*another name for Apollo, the Greek god of the sun.

Spring Haiku

I'M optimistic;
like a brand new tennis ball,
everything's chartreuse.

Dean Robbins

Poe Valley

FROM where we sat the lake below
shone verdant in the midday sun,
as if the mossy forest glow
was not a simple reflection

of the surrounding wealth of trees,
but something spread throughout the deep;
much more than what the surface sees,
and what the water means to keep.

Stone Wall

For Dale and Sis

GIVE me a seat near an old stone wall
    in a meadow stretching far
to a copse of trees where songbirds call
    and the deer and pheasant are;

where a creek fed from a mountain stream
    winds its way o'er polished stone,
and a butter knife breeze spreads a seam
    through a field no more mown.

Give me a seat near an old stone wall,
    whether bound'ry or the last
of an aged barn that once stood tall
    as the hay wagons rolled past.

Let seasons change and time crumble all
    that foundations underlie.
Give me a seat near an old stone wall
    and the words to mark it by.

Ben Grinberg

NYC

STANDING monolithic lights
Bless the pavement with their shine
Between the tall buildings' heights
Are the bleak, stiff human lines.
Faceless faces, hurried steps
Off to what home do they rush?
Every moment: lust or threat.
Every thought: "this costs how much?"
Yet, to tie life's fabric tight:
Virtuousness, all it takes.
And to make one's heart/mind light:
Moral codes life joyous make.
And the mass of concrete gray,
And the mass of flesh and stress,
Will become a fairytale
Of harvesting righteousness.

The Path of Self-Cultivation

EVERYONE around you
Drowning day and night
Everyone's got problems
But fails to make it right.

Their aching minds in worry
For how to earn a cent.
And when this life is over,
Just illness and regret.

"What's the use of building
A ship you know will sink,"
Say Buddhists in reference to
Life passing in a blink.

But followers of Dafa*,
You see it in their eyes
They've found this life's meaning,
In Zhen-Shan-Ren it lies.

The path of cultivation
Can truly set you free
Of endless incarnation
Of stress, disease, and greed.

For Zhen-Shan-Ren is what is good
And new worlds wait to hear your voice:
There is Law in the universe,
There is a "Right," you have a choice.

Chinese for "the Great Way"

Valerie Dohren

Beauty

I SAW the face of beauty fixed
   Upon the rising sun
Beyond all mortal compliment
   Her loveliness there shone

Within the constellations set
   Against the heav'nly realm
She glittered 'cross the universe
   My heart to overwhelm

The Seven Sisters ne'er could light
   All heaven like her smile
Nor Aphrodite's sweetest face
   The spirit to beguile

Then here beneath the starry dome
   She rests upon the land
Encaptured by the glist'ning streams
   And meadows, broadly spanned

For lying thus in fields of green
   With flowers in her hair
The benediction of her charms
   Is full beyond compare

She dances like a pearly wraith
   Upon the crested waves
So comely bound in all that which
   Imagination craves

Her voice is likened to the song
   The Mousai sing at dawn

And sunlight does her aspect grace
  In fields of golden corn

May beauty steal my eyes away
  From all in darkness veiled
And grant to me her precious gift
  'Gainst which all else is paled

O beauty shall you hearken thus
  My joy forever be
For beauty dwells within the soul
  As beauty is to me

Ellen Lou

Ode to New Beginnings

AS the leaves whither and fall away
The sun sleeps in and hides all day.
Days get shorter as time flies by,
The year has had its last reprise;
A new beginning awaits the close,
Where it will take us nobody knows.

Section II

Humor &
Children's Poetry

"Cobbler Studying Doll's Shoe," Norman Rockwell, 1921.

Damian Robin

A Bit of a Giggle-bite

I'VE had some poems I could submit
but now I've got behind a bit,
they're packed inside the silent hive
of a sev'ral-year-old, old hard drive

tho' un-backed-up, their form survives
in sev'ral forms of after-lives,
some stuck fast inside the lump
that's hard as nails and gives me stump

my teeth aren't hard enough to bite
just so hard and just so right
to get beneath the metal case
and reach the sweet of the database

where, with neat and gnarring grinds,
I could taste those still-there finds
and turn them on the tip of my tongue
to you, as tho' they were still young

"not to worry" and "never mind,"
the uni-verse can give in kind –
I've found, if thoughts are clear and clean,
hearts make good the old has-been

and friends tell me I can reclaim
what may seem lost in my mem'ry frame,
that what went off may come back on
[smiley face emoticon]

Bruce Dale Wise

A Guy Flopped Out upon a Tile Floor

By Rudi E. Welec, "Abs."

HE lay back down on the ceramic tiles,
his right hand balanced on the surface face.
Though sprawled upon that solid plane, he smiled,
relaxed and pleased, upon that hard, flat place.
He put his right hand underneath his leg,
despite his situation on the floor,
there laughing at himself, a cheerful egg,
insinuating he was good for more.
Sometimes one can let everything just go,
and savor, momentarily, mishaps.
Sometimes it's good enough to grin and glow;
one can still be content in a collapse.
That guy reminded me there's more to life
than struggle, strain, the strenuous, and strife.

The Little Kindnesses

By Bic Uwel, "Erased"

"…that best portion of a good man's life;
His little, nameless, unremembered acts
Of kindness and of love."
—William Wordsworth, Tintern Abbey

AT any time in life, the little kindnesses occur.
Somebody greets you with a smile brightening "Yes, sir!"
One store clerk reassures you at some absent-minded act;
another adds an unasked coupon to subtract the sum.
A courteous gas station aide politely pumps your gas,
and tells you this is a good day, while you sit on your ass.

How beautiful the morning is when someone's kind to you.
It makes you fall in love with life. It makes you feel new.
A sparkle in a worker's eye is captivating too.
How gorgeous is life when it's flowing flawlessly. "Thank you."

Kilmer Remilk

By Wic E. Ruse Blade

After Joyce Kilmer

I KNOW that I shall never see
a poem lovely as a tree;
nor shall I ever come to know
a tree that talks or thinks to go.

Andrew Joseph

Dihydrogen Monoxide

A MYSTERIOUS substance is ruling our lives.
It flows through our oceans and floats in our skies.
"It's good for you," cries four docs out of five.
It will keep your skin young for the rest of your life.
It will grow your corn tall and make your kids bright.
It will keep your drinks cold and improve your sight.
Believe me my friends, don't be fooled by the hype.
There is something about this that does not seem right.
Why would the great praises of this stuff be sung?
When you breathe in too much, it can swell in your lungs.
When frozen it's deadly, an Antarctic knife.
When used in some torture, they beg for their life.
So my dear friends I beg you, don't fall for their ruse
and as for myself I don't have to choose.
For I shall not be a mere sheep led to slaughter
Because I always prefer my whiskey to water.

Mike Alexander

The Gospel According to Hoffman-Laroche

A Villanelle

TELL me why the patient is still crying.
What pharmaceuticals? pain pills? barbiturates?
What pretties has the doctor been supplying?

Finish the prescription. Don't give up trying
the newest, truest of amalgamates.
Tell me why the patient is still crying.

Xanax will put you down when you are flying,
while Ecstasy delivers altered states.
What pretties has the doctor been supplying?

Whatever truths you cannot help denying
let Sodium pentothal unlatch the gates.
Tell me why the patient is still crying.

One dosage is for selling, one for buying,
Rohypnol for those reluctant dates.
What pretties has the doctor been supplying?

Tell me what you dole out to the dying.
What paradise or punishment awaits?
Tell me why. The patient is still crying.
What pretties has the doctor been supplying?

Ken Kenigsberg

The Battleground

THE slashing blades strike fierce and deep
The newly stricken fall down in heaps.
In vain: the foe storms back enraged,
The scythe-like swords remain engaged.

The rampaging hordes beat with passion;
Blade-wielders reply in their own fashion.
Undaunted, the enemy tries once more,
The swords, unstinting, produce more gore.

Midst all the blind, untrammeled fury:
No truce; no peace; no judge or jury.
No quarter given and none received
Is all the mad ones could conceive.

At last, Thor, god of heaven has been sated.
The roiling thunder stills; abated.
Long sought peace returns to earth
And wipers return to windshield berths.

Troy Camplin

A Health Insurance Limerick

THE cost of insurance was such
Its price I could sadly not touch —
So I gave all of that
To a young bureaucrat
And now it costs three times as much!

Reid McGrath

The Little Vector

A Ten-nos*

MY knee is like a cantaloupe: I am a humbled man.
It seems brutal that you are a part of the Master Plan.
The Desert States have scorpions; the South has rattlesnakes;
Australia and hot Africa have beasts within their brakes.
The Sea has sharks, the North has grizz, Islands have weird spiders;
while those in Northern Asia have Siberian tigers.
The Amazon has piranhas and the black caiman too.
Here in the Hudson Valley we are mostly plagued by you.
Because you're small, you are a threat; your bite won't even prick.
If left unchecked: your Lyme could kill. You are a bloody Tick!

**A ten-nos, the word sonnet written backwards, is a poem of ten lines
(five couplets) of iambic heptameter created by Bruce Dale Wise. A sonnet
is frequently 14 lines of 10 syllables; a ten-nos is 10 lines of 14 syllables.*

Janice Canerdy

What Robert Burns Might Say Today

O MY TV's had a gray, gray screen
  Since it blew up last June.
The radio plays no melody.
  The piano's out of tune.
Alas! My iPod's ceased to work.
  My laptop's gone kaput.
My car just died a violent death,
  And now I am on foot.
When HBO plays great, my dears,
  When car and gadgets run,
I'll pay thy exorbitant fees, my dears;
  Then we'll all be having fun.
So fare thee well, my saviors dear.
  I'll call thee in a while.
Take care of these, young fix-it men.
  They're really worth a pile!

Death by Animated Sponge

"MORE SpongeBob, Mimi"–this I hear
  a dozen times a day.
How much more can I stand to see?
  No more of this, I pray!
I turn the TV off and run
  to fetch his favorite toys.
When he says, "Spongebob's much more fun,"
  I must seek other ploys.
"A Krabby Patty's what I'd like,"
  he says of noontime's meal.
The common lunch I fix the tyke,
  he eyes with little zeal.
The Krusty Krab invades my sleep,

and Squidward haunts my dreams.
Those creatures from the ocean deep
    won't leave me be, it seems.
Can cartoon sponges start a trend
    of death by kiddie show?
If SpongeBob's laugh can cause the end,
    I'll be the first to go.

Jane Blanchard

Yin and Yang

"HELLO, again!"
the sun does say
when rising on
a morn in May.

"Thanks for the break,"
replies the moon.
"I need to go
to bed quite soon."

The sun then bids,
"Don't fade so fast!
Why can't you get
your light to last?"

The moon retorts,
"Fine talk from one
who sets each night
when day is done."

To the Media of America

THE British are coming!
The whole fourth estate
Must wear what is smart
For William and Kate.

The British are coming!
Men, watch how you dress:
A jacket and tie
Should lead to success.

The British are coming!
So, ladies, look nice:
A suit, pants or skirt,
Would likely suffice.

The British are coming!
Shun clothes à la mode:
No denim, no fleece,
Could meet royal code.

The British are coming!
Three days at the most,
Don proper attire
Or end up as toast.

Jessica Hoard

Teddy

HIGGLEDY-piggledy
Theodore Roosevelt,
twenty-sixth president
of the U.S.

Nickname was "Teddy," which
led to the teddy bear,
which I still sleep with, at
times, I confess.

Scáth Beorh

Some People Say

SOME people say
that giraffes were petite
and they grew their necks out
to properly eat,
or they were once dinosaurs
who lost their wings.
But I know God makes
serendipitous things.

I Had A Pair

I HAD a pair of tennis shoes
who caught a cold and couldn't play,
therefore I tucked them into bed,
opened the window—sky was grey—
turned on the radio for them…
that's when my sneakers spoke:
"I'd like to lie here for a while
and listen to Baroque."

Scott M. Sparling

Salazar Sneed

SALAZAR Sneed was a man of great need
Who traded holey shoes for a pocket of beads.
With the beads he then went to the market and bought
A pancake pan that was cast iron wrought.
The pan he then gave with a wink and a smile
To an old doffer who, in return, gave him a file.
He traded the file at the jail to a bird
Who promised to give all his friends a good word.
The word was as good as the bird promised Sneed.
The bird's friend, farmer Ben, gave Sneed three bags of seed.
So Salazar took the seed to market place
which he traded for a jade banded mask for his face.
The mayor liked the mask, offered Sneed a flask
Of copper and silver, and then gave him a task.
He said "Bring you this flask to the old widow Wen,
And she will in turn give you a fat hen!"
With hen under arm Sneed then took to the docks
He gave that squawking hen to old Wen for a clock.
What a fine clock it was, made of gold bronze and copper
So Sneed made his way down the street to the cobbler.
The cobbler impressed, he decided to dress
Sneed in some new shoes so as you can guess
Salazer Sneed headed back toward his goal
With a smile on his face and two shoes without holes.

Evan Mantyk

The Kite

DIP and drop and flip and flop,
Riding high up to the top,
Sail and soar and flail and flow,
Through the wind that wildly blows,
Holding tight onto her kite
That in her hand seems to fight,
The little girl could not be
In any way more happy.
Her lofty thoughts, like the kite,
Climb up to the greatest height,
Dipping, dropping, flipping, flop,
Ridding, gliding, tippy top,
Sailing, soaring, flailing, flow,
Going, going, going, go!

The Bored Knight

A TIRED knight rode to his castle
After a long day of hassle.
He bowed to the land's king, his lord,
"My liege, I'm incredibly bored,
I'm more like a stupid monkey
Than protector of royalty
I stand there at the outer gate
Like moldy food that no one ate.
Please, send me on some noble quest
That my virtue heaven may test."

His lord replied, "Tell me good knight
Did you see a man of tall height
Who wore red, carried a sickle."

The knight gave his chin a tickle,
And replied, "There was some fellow,
Who had wanted to say hello
To someone he said that he knew;
I had no word to let him through
And sent him home, despite his plea.

The King cried: "He was sent to kill me,
An assassin dressed as farmer!
Without a dent in your armor,
You stopped him from his evil quest,
Fighting boredom, you passed the test!"

Section III

Persecution in China

"Unshakable Faith" by Ben Li, 2014. People in China today face repression of the basic human rights we enjoy. The persecution of the peaceful meditation practice, Falun Gong, also known as Falun Dafa, (depicted above) is emblematic of this repression. All people in China today are victims.

Darlene Wolenski

A Battle of Good versus Evil

I.

THE people of China in ancient times,
Knew good was blessed and evil was punished,
By Gods who observed all of their actions,
When they were virtuous their country flourished.

For five thousand years they led their lives,
Their history replete with much glory,
But when the last dynasty came to end,
China became a different story.

When the twentieth century started,
A red dragon rose from an evil pit.
Trying to destroy China's legacy,
Faith in the divine it would not permit.

People's lives were cast into darkness,
Mistrust and corruption infected the land,
Lives were lost, a legacy destroyed,
By the government's malicious command.

But the Gods still watched from heavens above,
Witnessing China's destruction and plight,
They knew this evil must no longer rule,
And the wrong must be set right.

II.

IN May of the year nineteen ninety-two,
Falun Dafa was made known to mankind.

It taught to be true, good and to endure,
It transformed the corrupt Chinese mind.

The disciples bloomed like golden flowers,
The practice was quick to spread far and wide,
All saw the power of Zhen, Shan, and Ren
For it was turning back the evil tide.

But the evil, oh how it seethed with hate,
Refused to accept the Gods' direction,
It could not withstand such righteous people,
Thus, it started a brutal persecution.

With a jealous heart and a poisoned mind,
It desired to root out or crush their will,
And if they stood up for what was correct,
It did not hesitate to maim or kill.

III.
BUT, the Falun Dafa practitioners,
Were like bright lotus flowers in the rain,
No matter how the harsh wind lashed or stung,
Their faithful and pure hearts withstood the strain.

When beaten and bruised, they stood straight and tall,
And treated their captors with compassion,
When their homes and money were snatched away,
They stood tall in an admirable fashion.

The red demon's crimes became only worse,
As it struggled to keep absolute grip,
It surpassed history's worst genocides,
The one to blame is its dictatorship.

It began a harvest of the organs,
A new and unseen level of slaughter,
Yet he who kills unjustly for profit
Just makes the flames of justice burn hotter.

In all the battles of good and evil,
Those who are villainous can never win,
For the divine are behind the righteous,
Whereas the heinous will pay for their sin.

Dafa practitioners around the globe,
Are exposing this dark persecution,
For all of the crimes it has ever done,
The red regime will face retribution.

This persecution is no modern myth,
It is happening before our eyes.
Will you tell right from wrong?
Or be fooled by Communist Party lies?

Abigail Zhong

My Friend

MY friend, she wears a hat with a red star
Delivered from a warehouse as a joke
She holds the Communist Manifesto
Reads words on which so many others choke
Talks of overthrowing the bourgeoisie
Our classmates laugh, they have never seen truth
My parents don't speak of their old country
Their bodies have scars left over from youth

My friend knows nothing of revolution
The blood and tears shed in Tiananmen Square
The starvation of the Great Leap Forward
She's never fled her home out of despair
Mao's image still rests on grandfather's wall
The tide not fully turned, old wounds not closed
Scholars are muzzled not sent to the fields
Today, basic freedom is still opposed

My friend and I read our history books
Millions of deaths fit on a single page
Where lives are not lives, but neat statistics
Distance is a privilege of our age
In China, the monuments still bear scars
The soil remains bloody under their feet
But the people are moving forward still
A new generation filling the street

Mike Ruskovich

The Greatest Wall of China

WHEN commerce comes before the human soul,
And speech is caged and liberty's confined,
While privacy's imprisoned by a goal
That values money more than any mind
Where freedom is the currency of choice,
Then more is ruined than the land and air—
Pollution stains the hopeful heart and voice
That speaks against oppression everywhere;
It stains the fabric stitched by brotherhood
And builds the kind of thick restrictive wall
That harbors hate, restraining all the good
We'd have to share if only walls could fall.
When politics make bricks of helping hands,
The worst and highest wall of all still stands.

Cathy Bryant

The Spirits of the Murdered Falun Gong Practitioners Will Endure

TRUTH, compassion and forbearance
were the touchstones of your good lives.
When weapons made their appearance
you met them with prayer, not with knives.
Your plight moves many adherents.
Regimes rise and fall; your light thrives.
Truth, compassion and forbearance
were the touchstones of your good lives.

Donna Nelesen

Crossing China

I.

ANXIETY and excitement, a strange mixture
Saturated me as I attempted to picture
Two days alone crossing China's famous Silk Road
Aboard a train, the local transportation mode.

I envisioned Genghis Khan, the bold conqueror,
His hordes creating chaos, dismantling order,
The reverse of Marco Polo, who united East
And West, with a winding land route, restoring peace.

But most vivid in my mind's eye are windswept faces
Of silk traders plodding across desolate places,
Their precious cargo wrapped in animal skin bundles
Accomplishing their enterprise with desert camels

Inching snail-like over unremitting sand dunes, thirsting
For an oasis to rise instantly from the earth.
The trading of silk wove distinct cultures together;
This coveted worm cocoon, this unlikely treasure.

II.

MY eyes scan a sea of heads converging toward
A solitary turnstile. Panic mounts, (good Lord!)
As I suddenly grasp, that I too, must crunch my way,
With suitcase growing larger, I enter the fray.

At once, I wished I were sizes smaller, like a bird,
Could magically propel myself gracefully upward
Soar over angled eyes growing round with wonder,
And land effortlessly on the train station platform.

Instead my tour guide clings tightly to my blouse sleeve,
Tussled by the tide, nearly drowned, with no reprieve,
We're expelled through the turnstile, past efficient armed
    guards,
Used to sorting the masses like dealing a deck of cards.

III.

MY guide says goodbye as I get ready to board
In two days, she has introduced me to her world
Dynasties, fine arts, cuisine and celebrated sites
With rehearsed, cautious words, forced to stifle her rights.

But in the station waiting room, sentences unravel
Expressing a forbidden hunger before I travel
She whispers, "Is there really a God who loves me?"
Too famished to remain silent, wanting to believe.

En route, I met many other hushed disclosures,
Intimacies shared with a concerned foreigner,
A young woman sadly grieves, wanting more children
Desires a large family, mourns what could have been.

Another gave birth twice, endured threats and a fine
A second-born grateful that her mother crossed the line,
Hiding the obvious from prying officials' eyes,
Moving from village to village, she wore a disguise.

Sympathy breaches any language barrier.
These experiences expressed to a near-stranger.
The women marvel at the novelty of meeting
Someone who has spent a lifetime speaking freely.

Damian Robin

A Reflection on the '89 Democracy Movement

THE gun is mightier than brush or pen.
This was proved to death in Tiananmen,
across Beijing and parts of China too
where pro-vote banners got a seeing to.
All around Beijing the bullets ran.
The Party stamped its point because it can.
Because there is no vote but Party force
and all the world defers to Party force.

The streets were cleared of pro-democracy
and so is China's in-house history.
It does report "the June fourth Incident,"
not words like "massacre" or "innocent,"
about that day in nineteen eighty-nine
when troops with clattered noises crossed a line.

Chinese Cameo 3

LAWYERS are articulate and bright.
They ask, they listen, they analyse, they write.
They marshal what there is to know—the facts—
of law—of precedent—of clients' acts—
to organize the information, state
the sequence of events, balance weight
of argument with evidence. They use
words to clarify and not confuse.
They want to get the facts right. So how come
one of China's top ten lawyers is dumb
and mumbling? It's not too simple to say
the bench that put this advocate away

is evil. Gao Zhisheng had done such good
it had to nip this mouthpiece in the bud.

Chinese Cameo 8*

ON one curtain in our new front room,
this awkward daub of paint looks like a womb,
a uterus with its fallopian
tubes, becalmed in muted retro tan
same as the flanking walls we have replenished,
which look much better now the detail's finished.

This current curtain mistake must be washed,
cleaned, got rid of, eradicated, quashed,
like a blood smudge on a prison wall
or "birthing room" where dun fluids fall
with a slop on a glist'ning bucket fetus
more than a million billion steps from us
where single children make a family
and gain good growth in Sino currency.

**Note: The Chinese regime has relaxed its one child
per couple policy to allow couples to have two children
if one of the couple was a single child. However,
forced abortions are still happening regularly.*

Chinese Cameo 10

IN educated spheres of influence
a lot is practical and common sense.
You cannot talk of love or truth or God
because, if not political, they're odd.

And "social good" means "mattered property"
not long-groomed graces like Propriety.
You cannot ask in rounded conversation
about a higher being or cultivation.

Waiting at a Bus Stop Under an Umbrella

On the Mass Protest in Hong Kong, Autumn 2014

THE pro-democracy tear-soaked bud
could burst into a petaled flower flood.

Protesters gorged the city like a sea
and said they're not against the CCP*,

that foreign power just a march away.
But that had been on public holiday.

Will central shops and businesses agree?
Now holidays are over there's the fee

for rent and wages, power, overheads;
and with no customers this payment spreads,

for how can customers come in and spend
if the city center's one dead end?

And, yes, they're paying for police to wait.
And just how long will foreign powers wait?

*The Chinese Communist Party. People, such as
protesters in Hong Kong, have mistakenly attempted to seek reform within the party.*

A Reflection on Hong Kong's Umbrella Movement

With Evan Mantyk

THOUGH tear gas spiraled through receding light
and wrung out tears and mangled up clear sight;
and though the bitter gas was spiked with hate,
the thin-clad crowd did not retaliate.

The death of freedom's closed in "legal" care
not the "Open fire!" on Tiananmen Square
where peaceful rules faced tanks in single file –
the communist regime has changed its style.

As this is not the mainland years ago
and news teams round the world appear to know,
the massacre has moved behind the scenes,
no daytime deaths will viral up our screens.

State slander and coercion choke Hong Kong
with hands as dark as used on Falun Gong.

Ron L. Hodges

Shadow of the Laogai*

IN the Laogai's shadow, the ghosts of China stir,
Unseen by dreaming eyes as golden currents blow
Across the sea. Our compassion seems to falter
In the Laogai's shadow.

As the Red rope tightens, prices fall like Harbin snow
Upon the Western coast. What need have we to censure,
Though, when from this system countless riches flow?

Millions of sacrifices on the Party altar,
Millions toiling in the secret places that we know—
Until our dormant hearts bestir, the ghosts will labor
In the Laogai's shadow.

Note: Laogai are labor camps that often force prisoners to create products for export to other country.

Evan Mantyk

The Day the Persecution Began

"THE year is 1999, July,
A king of terror would come from the sky,"
The Frenchman Nostradamus prophesized
Indeed, the red dragon in China flies.
It covers all in its violent shadow,
Into detention centers it throws
The practitioners of Falun Dafa,
The hardworking citizens of China.

The day is July 20th, the same day
That Nero's flames in Rome still licked and swayed,
The same red flames he would blame on Christians
And use to fuel bloody persecution.
Again, the noble-hearted followers
Of the Way and Truth are made to suffer,
Again, the scene obscured to those on earth
Like game pieces with a perspective dearth.
On atheism and unquestioned science,
On power, control, decades of pretense,
Was fed the bloated Communist Party,
And now it sees a fresh new enemy,
A way to prove its prowess, reclaim might,
To show its state-sponsored claws can still fight,
And destroy "superstitions" of the past,
And hide that its own ignorance is vast.

One hundred million placid adherents,
Who believe in Truth-Compassion-Forbearance,
(Their voyage began, seven years before,
In 1992, their sails first soared.
That's five hundred years after Columbus
Unveiled a great continent before us)

They embarked upon a spiritual journey
Of meditation and discovery.

Upon the relentless waves of hist'ry
And facing a dragon who breathes mis'ry
These unknown heroes are poised on time's crest,
Today, they must pass the evilest test.

LinkedIn's Censorship in China

LINKEDIN* connects people the world over,
Crafting a cozy café oceans wide
Where people's posts can sit with each other,
"Do coffee" without an eight-hour ride.

Yet, recently, when I was at LinkedIn,
I noticed something red in my chai tea;
It tasted of metal, horror and sin;
The creamer was puss oozing profusely

From a Tiananmen Square protester's arm,
Rotting away after twenty-five years,
From the communists' torturous harm
To Falun Gong, a hint of salty tears.

I spat out the nightmare, ran out the door,
"If this is censorship, I want no more!"

*Under pressure from the Communist regime in
China, LinkedIn banned content related to Falun
Gong, beginning last year.*

Reid McGrath

Lamenting Our Complicity in the Installation of Suicide Nets

I MET a "bum" outside an Apple store
holding a sign which read: "I'm taking bets."
"On what?" I said. "On something that'd abhor
maybe the most insensate, calloused vets."
I curiously said to tell me more.
He had no problem, being garrulous:
"In China, in the dorms, the employees
will jump the window to forget the fuss
of toiling with iPhones— O the bane
of treating people like robotic bees!
I bet that, from now on, you won't forget
the pain resultant from another's gain.
You will envision a suicide net
and you'll shop different cause we're all to blame."

Ellen Lou

Just a Dream

I.

YOU vowed to descend to the world below,
    In an agreement that was made.
To the mortal world others dared not go,
    Yet what would happen if you stayed?
A promise to save sentient beings,
    Empowered your hesitant heart.
Your compassion for all living things,
    Made you determined to depart.

Within the universe a point was set,
    To be the center of events.
To this point numerous immortals went,
    And have stayed there ever since.
Down in the world of man they were reborn,
    Uncertain if they would return.

II.

FIVE thousand years of civilization,
    Was the arrangement at the start.
A blueprint made for each situation,
    And China would be at the heart.
How many dynasties have come and gone?
    How many emperors deceased?
How many dictators have come along?
    How many heroes' breath have ceased?

Predestined relationships guide our fates,
    And conduct us on our journeys.
Every life we know not what awaits,
    And we leave them in a flurry.

Through millennia in this world of sin,
    Our intentions were forgotten.

III.

AFTER numberless reincarnations,
    We have advanced upon today.
What was it that prompted our creation?
    Only the Law can light the way.
The Great Law Wheel is today in motion,
    Saving all sentient beings.
Even with the Red Demon's commotion,
    Law disciples are not fleeing.

Now we must all fulfill our destinies,
    In the agreement that was made.
Don't wait until the great catastrophe,
    For by then it will be too late.
One day, this concludes, strange as it may seem,
    And you'll find this world just a dream.

James Sale

The Commissars Oppose Falun Gong

THEY were old, had lost their youth,
So, like the old, repressed the Truth.

They fumbled, rigid in expression,
So stiff – they lacked Compassion.

Their purpose was interference,
Lacking right Forbearance.

In all this, all they had lost:
Truth, Compassion, Forbearance –
No Tao, but stuck at their dead post,
Trapped without deliverance.

Bruce Dale Wise

610 Office
By Li "Web Crease" Du

610 is there
to take it down,
the Falun Gong,
that touches Dao.
It's clear to see
the dangers of
forbearance, truth,
compassion, love.

Note: The 610 Office, created on June 10 (6/10), 1999, is an extra-legal agency whose sole purpose is to persecute Falun Gong. The 610 Office has absolute power at each level of administration in the Party and its influence trumps that of all of China's other political and judicial organizations.

Th' Umbrella Revolution: Autumn 2014
By Lu "Reed ABCs" Wei

TEN thousand or more demonstrators occupy
the center of Hong Kong. With plastic raincoats, masks,
protective goggles, and umbrellas, they defy
the growing rays of communist demands and tasks.
Against the vetting, they protest with love and peace.
Like freedom in the middle of a storm, they bask.
But haters of democracy don't ever cease.
They wait as well, for their own moment in the sun.
They wait to take their city back, to clear their streets.
They wait to burn away the filth with gas and gun.
They wait to shine on this charade, to flout the sky
with clouds of pepper spray that sting the eyes and tongue.

Section IV

Great Culture

"Hector Admonishes Paris for His Softness and Exhorts Him to Go to War," by Johann Heinrich Wilhelm Tischbein, 1786

Reid McGrath

Three Trojan Perspectives
For E.E. Club Saw Reid

I. Priam, Returning to the Ramparts
HE'D never say it to my face and yet
I sense that Hector senses I'm washed up:
too old, too soft. Not that he is the pup
that sees for the first time his dad beset
with something he can't handle, can't repair—
No, that was long ago; I feel ancient.
I'm sick of war and I am impatient
for things to go back to the way they were…

Think of Agamemnon, Odysseus,
dexterous Diomedes, jacked Ajax,
AWOL Achilles, and Menelaus—
By Zeus! Who could watch? Paris is too lax,
Trojans all. The Achaean army'd be a dream
if only they had Hector on their team!

II. Paris, Back in His Bedroom
BECAUSE he never let me fight my fights—
too protective, he always interfered,
having an older brother's heart, he jeered
at me in private, but on public nights
painting Troy red, when we were fun and young,
and when some badger mocked or called me out,
I never even had the chance to shout
before big Hector, Priam's favorite son,

had pushed me back, and got into the face
of that poor fool—I've got a lover's soul,
not a fighter's. They call me a disgrace!
loathe me like Black Death, whereas he is "cool."

I know it all too well that I've been spoiled.
Helen smells this coward who's recoiled!

III. Hector, in Front of His Men, Kicking at the Dirt

IT'S ridiculous all the times he's quailed:
say when we'd got to wrestling round the shocks
of grain (for fun) or on the salty docks
of some sea-town where we, as kids, had sailed;
and where the local thugs, reeking of fish,
would test our guts when chap'rons let us be.
He's never had the right integrity;
and off he'd flit before they served a dish

of knuckled fist smushed in his pretty face.
He is a chicken whereas Menelaus
is like some redbone barking at the base
of a tall tree. My brother is a wuss,
who I thought changed, but again let me down.
Especially cause Troy is our hometown!

Lines Composed Before Finding the Society of Classical Poets

SAVANTS like to arrange their stars
and push their poets into piles:
marble-misers who assign the jars
according to the artists' styles.
They line them in their fusty den
when they deem an era's past,
and deign to burp them now and then,
but work to invent a "new" cast.
Classicists have since ceased to be,
and Rhyme is out of fashion now,
but she still moves me like the sea
rocks a sun-soaked splintered scow.
All good men have come from men,
like oaks which out the leafmeal sprout;
what once was old appears again:
It is an everlasting fount.

Kristina Ng

The Great Exhibition of 1851

I SAW a grand palace as sculpted by
the Genie of the Lamp, adorned with lights
so golden, as if it came from within.
I saw great achievements under the sky
of glass, soared to extraordinary heights:
a modern Tower of Babel, raised again!

I saw a celebrated elm, stood tall
at the core of the temporal greenhouse:
a sylvan beauty painfully retained.
I saw white statues, never cease to enthrall:
Venus and Cupid, the Queen and her spouse,
exalted was the monarchy who reigned!

I saw a massive throng, of all stations
of life—naive eyes on the odd displays,
worth the ransom of a rich merchant ship.
I saw for the first time, tribes from nations
beyond ours; queer were their garbs to my gaze,
strange were the sounds of tongues, splendidly mixed!

I witnessed a paradigm of novelty:
the herald of a new age of science,
the verge of an amazing odyssey
of inventions—the temple's true triumph!

Yet, it's just a fantastical escape
of paupers into the pompous parade.

Bruce Dale Wise

A Father's Poem

A Ten-nos

I HOPE your life will offer you new opportunities,
that you will find contentment in the choices that you seize.
Remember family's important. You can count on us,
especially when the way of life is hard and mountainous.
Remember to believe in goodness, when you're down and out.
Remember never to give in to misery and doubt.
Remember wisdom comes with love and flourishes in life,
but it takes strength for father, mother, husband, child or wife.
The world has enormous wealth, but it takes eyes to see...
that each of us is only part of all humanity.

The Truth James Foley Stood For

By Cid Wa'eeb El Sur

JAMES Foley, searching for the truth, a photo journalist,
was murdered in cold blood by a masked IS jihadist,
beheaded on a video in deserts of Iraq,
mercilessly, cruelly, by a killer dressed in black.
The guy who only wanted to expose the suffering
was executed brutally without a covering,
his evil butcher camouflaged behind a veiled cloth,
his vicious killer shrouded as a grim and reaping Goth,
believing in the triumph of a cult of hate and death.
The truth James Foley stood for is clearly under threat.

The Fireman

By Reid Wes Cuebal

I SAW the fireman next to a fire hydrant post.
He had connected up his hose. The place was hot as toast.
Bright orange flames were burning wildly out of control.
He took his hose and sprayed and sprayed. He sprayed with
   lots of soul.
He kept his hose secure and firm, so 'twould not move about.
What was the chance that he could put that blazing fire out?
The gushing, rushing, flushing force was more than most
   could take,
but sturdily he kept it up, though he began to bake.
He got so hot he thought he ought to back off from the heat,
but he would go until the job he worked on was complete.

Variation on a Theme of Archilochus*

By Ercules Edibwa

I MET him on the battlefield so far from anyone.
I could not help but feel fear. This would not be so fun.
I placed my back against a solid place safe and secure.
I had to have my back protected if I would endure.
He came at me with shield and lance, with fire in his eye.
He was both vile and violent, that fierce, determined guy.
I set my stance. My legs were firm. I would not yield an inch.
I could not help but feel the hand of fate begin to pinch.
I held my shield steadily before his coming lance;
however, he knocked it about. I only had my stance.
But I could not escape, backed in the corner as I was.
From off life's stem I fell, fast as a dandelion's fuzz.

*Archilochus was a Greek lyric poet known for reporting
on his own direct experience.

When I First Heard the Learn'd Astronomer

By I. E. Sbace Weruld

A counter to a Walt Whitman poem

WHEN I first heard the learn'd astronomer
explain his proofs and figures, and arrange
the particles of this vast universe,
I was excited; I was not estranged.
I truly loved his charts and diagrams.
They made the cosmos understandable,
as if I'd found new diamond diadems;
its violence explained, deep-endable.
Then felt I like Balboa. His design
then made the chaos, of this crazed place I'm
located in, seem ordered and divine,
here in this cool and mystical space-time.
In perfect silence I looked at the stars
in rivers of eternity's crossed bars.

I Saw a Giant Train

By Red Was Iceblue

I SAW a giant train come out of blue and purple light,
the colours of its cars, red, yellow, orange, black and white.
It seemed gargantuan and powerful, a forceful shape,
about to take the World on in one horrendous rape.
I saw a Christ-like figure standing on the station deck,
a T turned from technology, a knowledge out of Tech.
The two could not be further from each other in that space,
machine and man, th' ungodly and the spirit in one place.
I saw a cataclysmic vision painted on a page.
It seemed to speak succinctly for the Nightmare of our Age.

Ron L. Hodges

A Plea to Scylla

From Glaucus to the Six-headed Sea Monster

THE first sound you uttered was not a roar
or a hiss but a pure, welcoming cry
when you spilled like gold from life's treasure door.
Your beauty made all the witnesses sigh—
eternity gleamed in each priceless eye.
As you grew, no mortal flaw marked your skin.
The heavenly spark was but brightened by
your womanly bloom. You performed no sin.
My ill-fated love made your suffering begin.

In youth, you were not a cursed monster,
plucking men off ships like grapes from a vine.
You laughed in joy as you danced on the shore,
waves kissing your feet so dainty and fine.
When I saw you, I swore you must be mine,
so I asked you, fair maid, with me to stay—
allow me to be the priest of your shrine.
But my sea-green power scared you away,
and you fled like the sun at the death of a day.

You fled my domain, displacing my heart
from its home. I sank, a shell in the sea.
I could never now endure life apart,
so I sought the aid of the witch Circe.
This desperate choice caused much tragedy:
Enamored, she sought my love for her own;
repulsed, the cold witch determined that she
would make you pay for my love all alone.
For my wretched sin, you would be forced to atone.

You were no wretch when you stepped in the pool
to wash any trace dirt from a body

so pure. Yet the sorceress had been cruel.
She poisoned the sea with nightmarish glee,
making the flesh you submerged turn beastly.
Below your waist spread a serpentine skirt,
which twisted and writhed like an old, scraggly
flag. Though your body and limbs were not hurt,
the shock of this transmutation made you inert.

As you steeped inert in the toxic bath,
your feminine frame deformed to a snake,
sprouting six heads like a bouquet of wrath.
Worse than this shape, your pure heart grew opaque,
as you allowed the corruption to take
your soul. You became a monster inside;
clasping darkness made all humanness break.
Your soft beauty washed out with the noon tide,
yet it was your choice whether the good Scylla died.

Now, the Scylla I once loved is long dead.
Her successor waits with reptilian
hate, dreaming of meat on a bone-strewn bed.
Instead of a god, from whom she had run,
she shares life with a swirling sea coffin.
At one time, you deserved divine regard
when, child-like, you gamboled under the sun.
Within the beast must some spot glow unmarred…
With Jove's love, you can desert this ocean graveyard.

So, dear Scylla, we know all will face pain.
Some sadly, like you, must suffer much more.
But for your eternal comfort and gain,
I hope you will reform your heart's foul core.
Turn from your choice of service to rancor,
and call on God to blot out this dark spot,
on you his purifying mercy pour.
We cannot control the source of our lot—
We can choose to fight on or to let our life rot.

Susan Martin

Truth in Fairy Tales

*"If you want your children to be brilliant,
tell them fairy tales. If you want them
to be very brilliant, tell them even more
fairy tales."*
—*Albert Einstein*

OH, the magic of Once upon a Time,
an entryway to a world undiscovered,
a place where children's dreams are recovered
of antic creatures who lived before time.
Threats of goblins who over them hover,
ogres and trolls who hide in the slime.
Yet nightmares o'recome by sweet dreams sublime.
Fairy godmother waits undercover
to help every child overcome fears.
She shows the way to navigate strife
and make greed and selfishness disappear,
for good will triumph, though evil is rife.
All a child must do is persevere.
Happily ever after, then, for life.

Clinton Van Inman

Cynthia Moon

GO drag your white skull before blind seas
That tumble dazed to your mono-eyed magic
Go string the treadmill tides around the poles
And make all starry lovers pale and sick

Go tell Neptune when the night is through
Charm him too with your waxing and waning
Awaken the Triton and all your mermaids too
Let them revel in your nocturnal wandering

But you can't catch me with those half smiles
As your borrowed brilliance exposes you
I have seen how your darker side beguiles
As I learned too late that you are never true

Go charm some other star struck rhapsodist
Lure him too into your midnight mist.

Firestone Feinberg

Ashamed I Will No Longer Be

ASHAMED I will no longer be
To write an older poetry —
I have the right to reach for rhyme
And make the most of measured time —

While looked upon I am with scorn —
And ridiculed — as per fashion —
I recall many others torn
Away from their deep heart's passion

By an ignorant and cruel crowd
Who spew the usual nonsense
Deriding us; as if license
To judge was just to them allowed.

Now suddenly my sight comes clear:
What motivates these men is fear!
Takes courage to defy the norm —
And courage takes a frightful form.

Mandy Moe Pwint Tu

To Wordsworth

WORDSWORTH, I pray thee, return to this mortal land,
Heaven can spare thee. The angels will understand.
   Earth has greater need of thee.

Thine words are read, but no longer heeded;
Humanity is cold; into "reason" receded.
There is no living voice as loud to awaken
These "logical" hearts; whom thought has forsaken.
They desire truth, but they decide it;
They desire beauty, and they design it.
The world is cold, so grey and dark now;
Wordsworth, I pray thee, liven it somehow.

Grasp a secret from the whispering trees
Capture an echo from the roaring seas,
Find a dewdrop on a budding rose
And tell them of these, that they shall know.
Teach them to marvel at the butterfly,
Which sleeps a worm, and wakens to the sky;
Remind them of beauty in the mundane,
Bid them to rescue that which might not remain.

Give them a song that they must listen,
Hand them a story from the stars that glisten;
Whisper to them an Elysian verse
That mayhap Keats had oft rehearsed:
Show them a dream that they will not abandon,
Write them a skyline, a broader horizon;
Learn them to see with enlightened eyes
That they release contented sighs.

So Wordsworth, I pray thee, return to this mortal land –
Heaven can spare thee. The angels will understand.
   Earth has greater need of thee.

James Sale

Apollo Builds Troy with His Lyre

A MIRACLE, how else to say it then?
At first, but ground, absolutely nothing there,
A river meandering by, some cattle, gorse,
Nettle and herbs whose use proved no sure cure.

Then, as if by magic, he stood majestic, by –
Conjured from out thin air his being gainsaid
Something – at first a stone, and then a column.
Up, up, it went as if to spear the sky:
A point, a pinnacle to span the vacuum

Between earth and heaven; and how he shone,
How bright his helmet, and how his shield hung;
But nothing compared with his sublime lyre:
The tune he plucked – to which his voice, soft, sang.

Incredible, the god Apollo before
The wall that rose visible each note he played:
Coming into being that which was not –
The whole of Troy, that destiny long delayed.

And the god's eyes glittered as they saw too
What only he could in the long before.
Completed, topless towers standing proud.
How long? 9, 11 minutes tops? Who's sure?

Only as the city took its rising shape
And the great god basked in self-adulation,
His dawning eyes wavered, once, as he felt
One fearful tear – and whither its destination.

Noah Survives Cancer

HE hammered on: no other way
It seemed to him to miss the storm;
And all the while they ate and drank,
Got married too, and all seemed calm.

They heard him hammer planks and knew
Another nail stuck in the hulk
That was a coffin which never would
Float for all he might do, or talk.

They laughed, why would they not? What folly
Is in the heart of man, and reigns –
Until a day come, more like night,
A pitter of unfamiliar rains?

He shut the hatch down; they took cover,
Certain as time was it would soon,
Like this interrupt, blip, be over:
Three fifty days, no sun, no moon.

Storm? You could call it that – more like
The great titan Typhon's pursuit
Of Zeus and all living things:
Life's orchestra now just one flute.

As he emerged into a world
He had not imagined before,
So unlike the one he had left,
He blinked. Had he survived for sure?

Nothing would ever be the same
Again; there would be no return;
Though, note, how grateful Noah was
To see light, there while his tears burn

And burn.

Robert King

Where Are We When We Are Not?

WHERE are we when we are not?
Why right here in what we wrote
Can writing be death's antidote?
Ah! Tis good art that survives
Good art immortality gives
Through bad art no one lives
Write badly and burn in hell

Heaven's for those who've written well
For most of us, only time will tell.

Mark J. Mitchell

French Suites

EACH keystroke is precise, clear as a verb
Untouched by modifiers. Sharps and flats
Are reliable as death, the light trills
All mapped out. This strict staff allows no room
For cadenzas. Play it as he wrote it.
Still, out of all that, out of each note hit,
A lyric grows. It approaches dance. Tunes
Float over measure. Hear the absence of frills,
The Protestant neatness of mind—and that's
All the truth in the music you just heard.

Michael Curtis

Courage

For Roibert a Briuis; Robert the Bruce,
King of Scotland (1274 – 1329)

I SAW a tiny spider spin a web
Within my humble hut between two beams.
He tried to throw a thread across, it ebbed
Away. He did not have the will, it seemed.
And then the tiny spider tried again,
Again he failed to reach the other side.
Five times the spider threw his thread, and then,
On the next try he conquered the divide.

With each attempt to win we gather strength.
We brace the will with failure and defeat.
We forge desire to win, we win at length.
We stretch our arms to win at war; we meet
Today a mighty army on the field:
The tiny spider taught me, "Never yield."

Neal Dachstadter

Fathers and Grandfathers

WHEN we see our Brethren bold,
Reach the age called Growing Old,
Men grow thoughtful, mind afire,
With the echoes of a Sire.

Working, eating, drinking, they,
Striding through their noontide-day,
With a stately, decent air,
That within the lion's lair

Stood with strength, and finding grace,
Prompting harm to mind its place,
Carved the wilds a kindly home,
Brightly shining 'mid the gloam.

Through mist of hazy time we see
With only memories of his knee,
The Fathers, who we'd strain to be,
Yea sometimes ought to, 'mid a sea

Of current streams, endeavors lost,
Facades whose worth but failed the cost.
I'll be like Padre. Perfect? Nay,
Just better than some foolish way.

Somnolence

BETWEEN the pillow and my head,
There dwells a place of words unread,
When book still stands upon my chest;
I know not how-long. 'Tis my salon.
A moment passed while word and page,
They slowed, like scripted plots a-stage,
And golden hues metastasized,
Decreasing motion, heady potion.
Long my day of toil did crest,
Walking brisk to help my best
Of thought to stir, some time to save,
The work all done, my room has won.
At last, old friend, all day forsook,
Now drowse I, slightly toward your book.
No bore: thou nightly, lovely drunk!
My bottle, word. My lust, unstirred.
Gymnastic-like, I stretch to greet
A second pillow, cool to meet
My elbow, right, that rests in peace.
To die this way? I cannot say.
To live eternal soaring high,
To reach the restful salon nigh
To God, the giver of the nod.
To gentle word, though yet unheard.

Duck Over Tahoe

WINTER ray of setting Sol,
Minted bay with silver pall
And water, gray as ashen sky,
Fraught with play and splashing nigh.

While the sun upon thee sets,
Dun and green, thy shadows get
Upon the strand till morning gleam;
Supper grand before me steams.

Section V

Essays & Translations

"Archimedes Thoughtful" by Domenico Fetti, 1620.

James Sale

To Rhyme or Not to Rhyme?

IMAGINE that you were lost in a wilderness and had to find your way out. Fortunately, you have with you a number of things, or tools if you will. In the first instance you have a kitbag, which is itself useful. Within it are various articles: a bottle of water, a knife, fork and spoon, a map, lighter fuel, matches, a compass, a chocolate bar, some rope, scissors, a can opener, a wrap-up plastic raincoat, and a few more pieces too, like the watch on your wrist. The question I would ask you is simply this: would you, therefore, given that you are lost and are not sure where or how far the next safe port of call is, jettison any of these items or tools? Would you say, this item is irrelevant, and I don't need it – I'll never need it – get rid of it? And further, when you are safely back home and start writing of your experiences, will you be prescribing to other travelers in the wilderness: you must never take a bottle of water with you – it's stupid, it's cheating, it's pointless? Or, argue having a map with you means that you are not really lost, so you are not really making a journey?

Sound somewhat fanciful? Not really, for this is precisely what happens in all areas of modern art, and especially poetry. We have three thousand years of tradition which has established a very useful toolkit in the armoury of poetry (and read the same for art and music). Techniques like meter and rhythm, using rhetorical devices such as onomatopoeia, metaphor, simile, allusion, anaphora and so on have been well established for millennia. And the reason for this is clear: these techniques, used judiciously, work! They create appropriate emotional (primarily) and intellectual effects in the listeners and readers of the work.

In English poetry rhyme is a special example of one such special effect. In fact rhyme is so ubiquitous that some less informed people seem to think that poetry is just that: rhymed couplets. But because some less informed people think erroneously about this topic does not invalidate its force. The truth is that rhyme is a massively powerful adjunct of poetry and this is demonstrated in two ways in the English-speaking world: first, children universally love nursery rhymes, and such rhymes are a brilliant device for aiding memory and recall. But second, advertising itself regularly uses rhyme – why? Because it works. An adult in England only has to think of one of the most memorable ads of the last 40 years: "A Mars a day/Helps you work, rest and play." We get it and the message embeds itself in our consciousness.

Why, then, for heaven's sake do we constantly get a stream of wannabe poets denigrating and banning rhyme, as if the use of rhyme were something no real poet would ever do? On the contrary, all significant poets have used it, and the very greatest poets do it a lot: Spenser, Shakespeare, Milton, Keats, Yeats – need I go on? Even the high apostle of free verse, T.S. Eliot, did quite a bit of it!

Of course, rhyming badly is not good. William McGonagall has become a by-word for bad poetry in which meaning has been wrenched by the necessity to find rhyme words. This, in his case, however, has become comical – people still want to read him for the pleasure of the forced rhymes. And here's the weird thing: I would predict more people read and enjoy McGonagall for all its incompetence (there is still a pleasure to be had in rhyme!) than ever read those stalwarts of serious "free verse": the "Howl" and the "Paterson" and all this shapeless stuff that drones on in its own self-importance.

There is, as I discovered recently in a debate, a vociferous number of people for whom poetry is not poetry at all, but a political act. For them, rhyme is some sort of bondage (and that of course has a creditable heritage in Milton's eschewing rhyme in order to write *Paradise Lost*) and they need to be "free" to write whatever comes into their minds as it comes without any sense of form or structure or device or technique or tools. And the result, of course, is that they don't write poetry at all, although they promote it as such. And they never improve. No verse is free, said T.S. Eliot, for the man who wants to do a good job. They just do not get—and cannot discipline themselves to study and practice—that the tools, the techniques are the very way we find our way out of the wilderness of emotional chaos (which is really their "freedom") and get to the land of true meaning, which is our home.

All this requires patience, study and craft. But all politics is too short-term for that – we want our freedom and we want it now:

look at this scribble – it's art! *Right?* We need to move on from this infantilism. Rhyme is not necessary for poetry; but rhyme is an amazingly powerful technique when used appropriately and properly, and understanding the various aspects of rhyme which are possible is itself an education. So let's not be put down by these political activists proclaiming "freedom" and who the while are wasting poetry with their wanton graffiti. Use rhyme when you want to – you know, it can sound so good!

Translations

Ascending the Phoenix Terrace in Jinling

By Li Bai (701-762)
Translation by Evan Mantyk and Chunlin Li

PHOENIX roamed here four hundred years ago,
A sign of the enchantment that once thrived;
Such emptiness now, no more feathers flow,
A lonely river is all that's survived.

The lush garden of the grand Wu Palace
Is buried there beneath some nameless brush;
What's left of the Jin court's elegance?
Just those mounds of ancient decomposed mush!

The Three Mountains disappear into sky,
Aloof and azure, from whence egrets dive
To a remote river isle, safe and dry,
Two streams of the Yangtze onward strive.

My mind drifts to Chang'an, so far from here
And the Emperor whose fate is unclear;
I've heard dark clouds obscure his brilliant sky;
I wish, to his aid, a phoenix would fly.

Yellow Crane Tower

By Cui Hao (704-754)
Translation by Evan Mantyk and Chunlin Li

A TAOIST immortal once left this place,
Riding on the back of a yellow crane.

Lighter than the air, he left not a trace;
Only Yellow Crane Tower does remain.

The yellow crane, once gone, never returned;
One thousand years have flown by without wings.
The listless clouds for company have yearned,
But it's something empty sky never brings.

Sunshine illumines the trees to the north
Of the Han River's crystalline water.
From the verdant grass, sweet fragrance pours forth
As parrots on river islands gather.

Shadows from below creep up the tower;
I've no crane to ride at this late hour;
Which way leads to my home? I do not know,
O, misty river, I've so far to go!

Holy Sonnet 19

By John Donne (1572-1631)
Translation into modern English by Reid McGrath

OH, to challenge me, two selves meet in one:
Inconstancy ironically begets
a constant habit. Like a reed that lets
the wind sway it, willy-nilly, I shun
yesterday's vows; I'm like a hypocrite
who fesses-up, then walks outside to sin.
One half is hot, one half is cold, within
this stubborn mule who loves, then loathes, the bit.
I pray; I'm mute; I'm chaste; I'm lewd; I pine
for Life, not Heaven; but then here today
I see my fatal error and I pray
for all of His forgiveness one more time.
I'm like a fever, and yet I still know,
my best days are when my head is bent low.

L'infinito

By Giacomo Leopardi (1798-1837)
Translation by Reid McGrath

THESE hills are dear to me as they're lonely;
dear is this hedgerow, which cuts off the view
of the horizon, because here I see
sitting, gazing, with my mind's eye, the true—
the infinite spaces, depthless repose,
till what I feel is nearly fear. The breeze
blowing in these branches, the leafy clothes—
I start to compare—of the rustling trees—
with endless stillness, and the setting sun,
the eternal peace and dead seasons passed,
juxtaposed with the present, lively one,
remind me that mere earthly things don't last.
Thus my mind: in stillness, then noise, goes round,
and flounders sweetly, in this sea I've found.

Sonnet 55 of Eugene Onegin

By Alexander Pushkin (1799-1837)
Translation by Reid McGrath

I AM made to live in some calm county.
I relish a rural tranquility.
When all's quiet, I'm rich with a bounty
I must pay for my creativity.
I'm simply entertained, I dabble
farming, gardening. I hear the babble
of flowered streams or of lake-waves lapping
while I'm "Dol-ce far nien-te"* tapping
out on my fingers either warm or cold.
These are blithe hours, happily "squandered."
I sleep a little; I read. I've pondered
how I've given up the pursuit of Gold.

In my leisured prime, have I not tasted
the country's flavor that others wasted?

*An old Italian phrase that literally means
"sweet doing nothing"

Twenty Years Later

By János Vajda (1827–1897)
Translation by Zsuzsanna Ozsváth and Frederick Turner

LIKE snow on Mont Blanc's distant crest,
That neither sun nor wind may harm,
My unvexed heart now lies at rest,
Inflamed by no new passion's charm.

Round me a myriad stars contend
Which casts the most flirtatious glow,
And on my head their bright rays bend,
Yet never do I melt or flow.

But sometimes on a silent night,
In lonely dreamings, half-awake,
Your swanlike image floats, so white,
On vanished youth's enchanted lake.

And then my heart flares up again,
As after a long winter's night
Mont Blanc's eternal snowfields, when
The rising sun turns them to light . . .

A Soldier's Song, 1589

In Laudem Confiniorem
To the melody of "Only Sorrow"
By Bálint Balassi (1554–1594) /
Translation by Zsuzsanna Ozsváth and Frederick Turner

KNIGHTS-at-arms, tell me where there is a place more fair
  than the far fields of the Pale?
When soft is the springtime, sweet the birds' singtime,
  over the hill and the dale;
All in heaven's favor receive the sweet savor,
  dewdrop and meadow and vale.

And the knight's heart is stirred by the fire of the word
  that the haughty foe draws near,
Pricked to more merit by the spur of his spirit,
  goes to his trial with good cheer;
Wounded yet ready, though his brow be all bloody,
  seizes and slays without fear.

Scarlet the guidons, bright heraldry gladdens
  on surcoat and standard below,
In the vanguard he races, the field's vast spaces
  courses, like wild winds that blow;
Gaily caparisoned, bright helms all garrisoned,
  plumed in their beauty they go.

On Saracen stallions they prance in battalions,
  hearing the blast of the horn,
While those who stood guard when the night watch was hard,
  dismounted, rest in the dawn:
In skirmish and night-fray unending well might they
  with watching be wearied and worn.

For the fame, for good name, and for honor's acclaim,
  they leave the world's joys behind,
Flower of humanity, pattern of chivalry,
  to all, the pure form of high mind;

And as falcons they soar over fields of grim war,
    unleashed to strike in the wind.

When they see the bold foe, in joy they Hollo!,
    cracked lances fly end over end,
And if things fall out ill in the field of the kill,
    rally without a command,
And mired in much blood oftentimes they make good,
    drive their pursuit from the land.

The great plains, the forest, the groves at their fairest,
    are their castle, so they deem;
The ambush at woodways, the struggle, the hard days
    are their groves of academe;
Their hunger in battle, the thirst, the hot rattle,
    pleasures to them well beseem.

Their joy in their labor's the blade of their sabers,
    the skull-splitting edge they try;
And bloody and wounded, and many confounded
    in battle, silent they lie;
And the beast's maw full often, and the bird's, is the coffin
    of those who in courage must die.

Young knights of the marches, no shame ever smirches
    the glory that ever is yours,
Whose fame and good name the world will acclaim
    to its farthest and noblest shores;
As the fruit to the tree, may Providence be
    a blessing to you in the wars!

Alexander Tames Bucephalus

Prose by Plutarch (46-120)
Translation by John Dryden (1631-1700)
Rhyme by Bruce Dale Wise

THESSALIAN Philonicus brought forth the horse,
Bucephalus, to Philip, offering to sell
that steed for thirteen talents; but when they, perforce,
went to the field, they found him unmanageable,
so vicious. When they tried to mount him, up he reared,
and would not then endure any attendant's try.
Considered useless and untractable, they steered
Bucephalus away. But Alexander, standing by,
said, "What an excellent horse do they lose for want
of boldness and address to manage such wildness."
His father Philip took no notice at the taunt;
but when his son repeated his vexatiousness,
his father Philip spoke. "Do you reproach those who
are older than yourself, as if you knew more, and
were better able to man him than they could do?"
"I could do better than the others," Alexander said. "And if you don't, what will you forfeit for
such rashness?" Philip asked. "I'll pay," his son replied,
"the whole price of the horse." At this the company
guffawed, and set the bet. Immediately he tried,
ran up to the horse, grabbed his bridle directly,
and turned him to the sun, having, it seems, observed
he was disturbed at his own shadow's motion's flow.
Then let him go a little forward, holding reins.
He stroked him gently when the horse started to grow
more fiery and eager. Then, upon no pains,
let fall his upper garment softly down, and with
one leap, securely mounted him. When seated, he
by little drew the bridle in and curbed his wrath
by neither striking him, nor spurring him. When he
discovered he was free of all rebellion, and
impatient for the course, he let him go full speed,
inciting him but now and then with a command

or urging him on forth, well-heeled or briskly kneed.
King Philip and his friends looked on in silent awe
and anxiousness for the result, till seeing him
turn at the end of his career, and come back strong,
rejoicing and triumphant in fine, pleasing whim
for what he'd done. All burst in acclamations of
applause, his father shedding heady tears of joy.
He kissed his son, who came down from the horse, in love;
and in his transport said these words unto his boy:
"My son, be on the look out for a kingdom that
is equal to and worthy of yourself, because I see
that Macedonia is far too small a land
for one who willingly seeks such extremity."

Poets

Alexander, Mike is an American poet who lives in Houston, Texas.

Balassi, Bálint was one of the greatest Hungarian poets of the Renaissance period. He was a baron and was known for his adventurous life.

Beorh, Scáth is a writer of Ulster and Cherokee ancestries whose books include the High Fantasy novel *Black Fox In Thin Places* (Emby Press, 2013), the story collections *Children & Other Wicked Things* (JWK Fiction, 2013) and *Always After Thieves Watch* (Wildside Press, 2010), the Fantasy novel *October House* (Emby Kids, 2015), and the poetic study *Dark Sayings Of Old* (JWK, 2013). Raised in New Orleans and West Florida, and having made trips to India and Ireland, he now makes a home with his joyful and imaginative wife Ember in a quaint "turn of the century" neighborhood on the Atlantic Coast of Florida.

Blanchard, Jane lives and writes in Georgia.

Bryant, Cathy. After studying philosophy at university, she worked as a civil servant, a sales assistant in a shoe shop and a childminder, among other jobs. Working around her disabilities, she writes whenever she can. Her current projects include a Jane Austen themed comedy novel. Cathy lives in Derbyshire, Great Britain.

Camplin, Troy is an author, poet, and interdisciplinary scholar living in Richardson, Texas.

Canerdy, Janice is a retired high-school English teacher living in Potts Camp, Mississippi.

Carr, Fern G. Z. is a member of and former Poet-in-Residence for the League of Canadian Poets. She composes and translates poetry in five languages. A 2013 Pushcart Prize nominee, Carr has been published extensively world-wide from Finland to the Seychelles.

Her poem, "I Am," was chosen by the Parliamentary Poet Laureate as Poem of the Month for Canada. Carr is thrilled to have one of her poems currently orbiting the planet Mars aboard NASA'S MAVEN spacecraft. Her website is www.ferngzcarr.com.

Cui, Hao was a leading poet during the Tang Dynasty, which is considered China's Golden Age for its flourishing culture and arts. He was a proponent of regulated verse.

Curtis, Michael has 40 years of professional experience in architecture, sculpture, and painting. He has taught and lectured at universities, colleges, and museums including The Institute of Classical Architecture and The National Gallery of Art. His paintings and sculptures are featured in over 300 private collections; his many public statues can be found in The Library of Congress, The Supreme Court, other public buildings and squares.

Dachstadter, Neal was born in Georgia not too far from his family's Hereford and Angus farm. He lived in Albany, Texas and Reno, Nevada before deploying as a Chaplain to Hawijah with the Oregon, Idaho and Montana National Guard in 2005. Neal is currently the "House Dad, Philosopher & Caretaker" of the Louisiana State Chapter of DKE in Baton Rouge.

Dohren, Valerie is a widowed mother of one daughter and a retired public employee in England.

Donne, John was a major English poet of the late Renaissance period. He is associated with a group known as the Metaphysical Poets. He served as a cleric in the Church of England.

Dryden, John was the greatest English poet of the Restoration period in the 17th century. He served as Poet Laureate of the United Kingdom.

Feinberg, Firestone is a poet living in New York City.

Grinberg, Ben is an ethnically Jewish poet born in the Soviet Union (Moldova) and living in Minneapolis, Minnesota. He studied at Boston University, at campuses in both Mexico and Taiwan, and received a self-designed B.A.: "Three Approaches to Reality: Philosophy, Psychology, and Chinese Religions." His colorful history includes wrestling, professionally acting, organic farming, yoga instruction, and time in a U.S. Army boot camp. He now writes for VisionTimes.com, a soon to be hugely popular viral news website.

Hoard, Jessica is a poet and actress living in Chicago. Her Twitter address is @jesshoard.

Hodges, Ron L. is a long-time English teacher, having taught at Oxford Academy in Cypress, California, for the past ten years. About a year ago he started writing poetry. He lives in Orange County, California with his wife and two sons.

Joseph, Andrew is an aspiring writer and poet from Lima, Ohio, where he lives with his wife Julie and four children.

Kenigsberg, Ken is a poet living on Long Island.

King, Robert is a retired lawyer and poet living in California. His website is theoryofpoetry.com He is sole Editor of a book on poetics, *Poetry is – José Garcia Villa's Philosophy of Poetry*, scheduled to be published this year by Ateneo de Manila University Press, Manila, Philippines, and to be distributed in the U.S. as well as the Philippines.

LeKane-Yentumi, Shari Jo lives in St. Louis, Missouri, where she writes poetry, prose and articles; specializes in literary criticism and non-profit matters. She has a B.A. in English, Spanish, and an M.A. in Spanish from Saint Louis University in Madrid and St. Louis. Since brain surgery, she volunteer teaches creative writing in a maximum security jail and works for civil rights attorneys. She completed a novel in verse, *Poem to Follow*, and is featured in several poetry anthologies. Her poetry has appeared in several literary magazines in the U.S., Canada, England, India, Ireland and Spain.

Leopardi, Giacomo was a major Italian poet and scholar of the early 19th century.

Li, Bai is considered one of the greatest poets in China's 5,000-year history. He wrote during the Tang Dynasty, which is considered China's Golden Age for its flourishing culture and arts.

Li, Chunlin is an assistant professor at Fei Tian College in upstate New York. He has a Ph.D. in Comparative Literature from the University of California, San Diego.

Lou, Ellen is a senior at Fei Tian Academy of the Arts, in upstate New York.

Mantyk, Evan is an English teacher in upstate New York, where he lives with his wife and two children. He is President of the Society.

Martin, Susan is a poet and retired English and Creative Writing Teacher living in New Jersey.

McGrath, Reid is a poet living in the Hudson Valley in New York. He is winner of First Prize in the Society's 2015 Competition

Mitchell, Mark J. studied writing with George Hitchcock, Barbara Hull and Raymond Carver at the University of California at Santa Cruz. He lives in San Francisco with his wife, the filmmaker, Joan Juster. He has two novels, *Knight Prisoner* (Vagabondage Press) and *A Book of Lost Songs* (Wild Child Publishing).

Nelesen, Donna received a B.A. in English from the University of Oregon, with a primary focus on creative writing, especially poetry. Two years ago, after a long hiatus from writing which included teaching, overseas travel, computer graphics work, and studies in forensic science, she returned to my former passion. She lives in Phoenix, Arizona. azpoet2015@cox.net

Ng, Kristina is a poet living in Malaysia.

Ozsváth, Zsuzsanna holds the Leah and Paul Lewis Chair of Holocaust Studies at the University of Texas at Dallas, where she is also director of the Ackerman Center for Holocaust Studies. Her book of translated Hungarian poetry is called *Light within the Shade: Eight Hundred Years of Hungarian Poetry.*

Plutarch was one of the great historians of ancient Rome.

Pushkin, Alexander was the leading poet, dramatist, and novelist of the Romantic period in Russia and considered one of Russia's greatest poets. His most enduring work, *Eugene Onegin*, is a novel in verse about a Russian dandy in and out of love.

Pwint Tu, Mandy Moe is a Burmese poet studying in Australia.

Robbins, Dean is a poet living in Pennsylvania. He can be found on Facebook at Dean Robbins' Poetry.

Robin, Damian lives in England. He works for an international newspaper and a bilingual magazine. He lives with his wife and three children. He won Second Place in the Society's 2014 Poetry Competition.

Ruskovich, Mike lives in Grangeville, Idaho. He taught high school English for thirty-six years. He and his wife have four children. He is winner of Third Prize in the Society's 2015 Competition.

Sale, James FRSA is a leading expert on motivation, and the creator and licensor of Motivational Maps worldwide. James has been writing poetry for over 40 years and has seven collections of poems published, including most recently, *Inside the Whale*, his metaphor for being in hospital and surviving cancer, which afflicted him in 2011. He can be found at www.jamessale.co.uk and contacted at james@motivational maps.com. He is the winner of Second Prize in the Society's 2015 Competition.

Smith, James is an Australian architect and photographer living in upstate New York.

Sparling, Scott M. is a poet and playwright with many poems in publication in various locations and many children's plays published by Meriwhether Publishing. He also works as a professional Children's entertainer doing Magic Shows, Balloon Animals and Trivia Contests. Scott Lives in Washington State with his wife and three kids.

Stratford, Meryl: Her chapbook, *The Magician's Daughter*, winner of the 2013 YellowJacket Prize for Florida Poets, is available from YellowJacket Press.

Turner, Frederick is an internationally known poet, lecturer, and scholar, and Founders Professor of Arts and Humanities at the University of Texas at Dallas. His book of translated Hungarian poetry is called *Light within the Shade: Eight Hundred Years of Hungarian Poetry.*

Vajda, Janos was a poet in the late Romantic period in Hungary.

Van Inman, Clinton was born at Walton-on-Thames, England in 1945 and graduated with a BA from San Diego State University in 1977. Currently, he is teaching high school in Tampa Bay where he lives with his wife, Elba.

Wise, Bruce Dale is a poet living in Washington State who often writes under anagrammatic pseudonyms. He won First Prize in the Society's 2014 Competition and is winner of Fourth Prize in the Society's 2015 Competition.

Wolenski, Darlene is a senior at Fei Tian Academy of the Arts, in upstate New York. She is the winner of the High School Prize in the Society's 2015 Competition.

Zhong, Abigail is a junior at Oxford Academy high school in southern California and President of the Poetry Club. She wants to pursue a career in medicine. She is the winner of the High School Prize in the Society's 2015 Competition.

Made in the USA
Charleston, SC
30 March 2015